Six Weeks

Six Weeks

Poems by
Richard Scarsbrook

TURNSTONE PRESS

Six Weeks
copyright © Richard Scarsbrook 2013

Turnstone Press
Artspace Building
206-100 Arthur Street
Winnipeg, MB
R3B 1H3 Canada
www.TurnstonePress.com

Turnstone Press gratefully acknowledges the assistance of the Canada Council for the Arts, the Manitoba Arts Council, the Government of Canada through the Canada Book Fund, and the Province of Manitoba through the Book Publishing Tax Credit and the Book Publisher Marketing Assistance Program.

Printed and bound in Canada by Friesens for Turnstone Press.

Library and Archives Canada Cataloguing in Publication

Scarsbrook, Richard, author
      Six weeks / Richard Scarsbrook.

Poems.
ISBN 978-0-88801-448-1 (pbk.)

      I. Title.

PS8587.C396S59 2013   C811'.54   C2013-903747-0

This book is for Bluebell.

Contents

Interlude: Equations

Vapour Trails

Six Weeks

Coming Attractions

Matinee

Gene Kelly and Leslie Caron
a pas de deux beneath Pont Neuf

Fred Astaire and Audrey Hepburn
at Le Caveau de la Huchette

you'll paint a nail-polish heart upon
a background of sky-blue glitter

I'll snap the lock on Pont des Arts
and smile for the tourist cameras

we will dance inside our room
at the end of Passage Jouffroy

and as sure as Eiffel's spotlight is
our own projector beam

we will meet atop another tower
like Cary Grant and Deborah Kerr

Accelerator

although some fool had stood you up that night
and I'd been dumped for an ex just a week before
despite December's slush and muck and greyness
all around

the sky in your eyes
summer blue as you arched
into a free fall and plunged
into me just like that

and suddenly I
        was sixteen again

                behind the wheel of my beloved heap

                   racing down a back road

                   lit only by moonlight

                   on the first night of the year

                   warm enough

                   to roll down the windows

                   and stick one arm out

                   into the moving world

Body Art

from her crimson-lacquered toe
a slingback dangles

the faerie on her ankle
is poised to soar

higher than the dragon
breathing fire on her shoulder

        her ring clinks the glass
        of double-helix effervescence

        from beneath her sweater's furrows
        a tiny leaf sprouts

he wonders: will you show me
the rest of your flower?

        I've got two, she whispers
        a bluebell on my breast

        and an orchid, planted
        in more sacred ground

        only my lovers get to see them

he ventures: can I see
just the bluebell, then?

        she leans forward on her elbows
        on the glass-topped table

        and says, you're persistent

Swirl

plastic banner flapping
inviting us in:
PATIO OPEN!
you'll like this place
you insist

leaning back in
that white plastic chair
inhaling deeply as if
exhaust fumes are
as sweet as the scent
of lilac trees back home
as if you've always been
this high-heeled city girl

my tongue spiralling through
a mouthful of ale
you kiss the lip
of that Pilsner glass
your gaze skyward like
you've seen all this before

swirl stick stirring
ice clinking along
with the chorus
of screeching
streetcar wheels
the echoed wail
of frantic sirens
the roar of
subway trains

rumbling up
through sidewalk grates
haggling, shouting
the swirl of
unlearned languages
surrounds me like
rushing water

a shivering feeling
this learning to swim

Contact

each time he tries to make
eye contact with
the others in the room
she

> (wearing
> vintage sixties dresses
> golden cuff bracelets
> sheer smoky stockings
> her hair done up like
> a Motown backup singer)

draws him in
and
his eyes will stray to hers
again
and again

> (later
> she will tell him
> blinking as she says it
> I dressed up for you
> I wanted you
> to notice)

one night
he will follow
her to the subway
small talk will be made
on the way, but
love will be made
with their eyes
as she
descends

    (it worked
    he will tell her
    I noticed)

Come with Me

weeks later, a drink
becomes many, and
she says, my father
is Irish
my mother, French

he sees the Irish in her eyes
and in that luscious lower lip
that even now, this early
he wants to suck between his own
eyes closed
no sight
only feel

I'm going to Ireland tomorrow
he blurts, want
to come
with me?

she would say yes, but
she doesn't have a passport
her suitcase isn't packed
and she's going to be hungover

yet
even now she wants
to come
with him

and now he wanders Dublin
alone but somehow with her
taking pictures of the things
he wishes they could share

En Français

months later
inside her
apartment with the painting
of Sacré Coeur in the hallway
just slightly to the east
in her bedroom he will see
the French in her body
the small, perfect breasts
red bullet nipples
ribs symmetric
muscled stomach
like the dancers
down Montmartre's slope
inside
the Moulin Rouge

Invitation
(Love Song #1)

you tell me
you grew up in a town
where smiles disguised intentions

you tell me
you were brought up in a house
where dreams were never mentioned

you imply
you can't distinguish
truth from invention

it seems that we grew up together
it seems that we're from different places
same town, same house, same runaround
same problems, different cases

this is an open invitation
to come as you are
no need to dress up or down
no need to make a reservation
to dance without light
to drink all the night
from the shadows

we can tango through
this rainy syncopation
with heartbeats as strong and steady
as ritual drums

this is your invitation
to come

Mixed Tape

sweating in Mount Pleasant
joking about phallic tombstones

trading mixed-tape CDS
that became our daily soundtracks

hanging at The Only
just like that Lowest of the Low song

taking pictures
of you taking pictures

two perfect leaves
for Mackenzie King and us

it wasn't one broken butterfly
it was two making love

Midnight in Paris
at a failing eighties multiplex

why I like Ally Sheedy
better than Molly Ringwald

a trip to the Candy Store
(insert double meaning here)

appearing in your dreams sometimes
the things you do in mine

the difference between a kiss goodbye
and a kiss goodnight

Neon Sin
(Lavender Blue #1)

stretched out like nothing
I ever could have pictured
each curve
each line,
each shadow
seems to quake, to shimmer like
rain beneath a streetlight

those wiry muscles in
your arms stretched tight
as hydro wires in winter
a white expanse
of milk-smooth belly
rises, an island
from beneath
a deep black sea

oldies play on
the bedside radio

> *Lavender blue, dilly-dilly*
> *Lavender green*
> *If I were king, dilly-dilly*
> *I'd need a queen*

what else can we do?

remind me that
the vibration
is an illusion
an afterthought
of the neon sign outside
and also that you're just a friend
and unavailable, too
though we didn't plan this hurricane, or
that there'd be just
one vacant room

I'll sit here in this chair and watch
the pink light skitter, nervous hands
across your outstretched form

if I smoked, I'd have a cigarette
to kill the taste of guilt

The Reasons Why

maybe I love you
because you love thunderstorms
backlit sunset clouds
like small apocalypses

maybe I love you
because you walk
through the golf course at midnight
(but not during the day because
of the plague
of golfers then)

maybe I love you because you leave
dandelions tied to my doorknob
strings of jute from
the frayed spot on your backpack
tied to the light above
the kitchen table, and blossoms
to dry like artefacts
atop my computer screen

maybe I love you because your name
means Queen and mine means King
(and the implications of meaning
are priceless)

maybe I love you because
you were born in the same month as I
and when we're together we mesh
like two gears with identical teeth
we spin in such a way that we
are really never sure
which one is driving
and who is being driven

and maybe I love you because
all this makes me think
that perhaps astrology is not such bunk
as I once thought it was
since we were born under the same sign
and, when you think of things that way
the years don't matter so much

maybe I love you because you could
be sitting on your bed right now
waist-deep in a shallow pool of blankets
in a swirl around your hips
like waves that have paused for breath
a notebook balanced on your knees
writing a poem just like this one
to give to me tomorrow
when you sneak in for
an hour or two

and maybe I love you because you let
yourself into my house
when I am not even there
with the key that I keep hidden
behind the door on a nail
you leave cookie crumbs and funny notes
for when I get home and you've already left
I tuck them away
like parchment quotes
from long-lost sages
(the notes, not the crumbs)

maybe
I love you because
you eat your cupcakes from the bottom up
saving the sweetest part for last
waiting for that final
cherry pop-rock burst
like the way that I am waiting for you
to stay for a whole night
sometime soon

maybe
I love you because
we once bought two goldfish together
you took them into the mall washroom
held them between your legs as you sat
and for the first time
I felt jealous
of fish in a plastic bag

and maybe
I love you because you picked stones
from the beach with me in June
inspecting each one as if it were
an opal
or a tiger eye
condemning to the brownish water
those judged less than unique
and later
you held the goldfish
flipping in your upturned palms
as I arranged those pebbles
at the bottom of the tank

maybe I
love you
because
of the bittersweet smell you leave behind
on the armrest of my well-travelled couch
when you fall asleep waiting for me to come home

maybe I
love you
because
you and I are both slender and tall
like reeds in a pond that bend
as the breeze is inclined to sway us

maybe I love you because of the way
your small perfect breast
fits neatly in
to the cleft in my chest
when we dance

and maybe I love you because we're even
dancing like this at all

(because we have to
kill the lights
and pull the shades
because you are supposed to be
somewhere else)

maybe
I love you because of the ring
my gold-ring grandmother gave to me
saying "save this for your Queen
when she comes"
you once tried it on
and it fit like a birthmark
and if you don't claim it
as your own
it will just stay locked away

or maybe
I love you because of the ring
my silver-ring grandmother gave to me
(the strongest woman I've ever known)
which also fit you
the way it fit her

or maybe
I love you because you lost
your rings on the beach one night
and though others who would have you
searched the beach with as much intent
it was I who found them
and gave them back

or
maybe I love you
just because you found me

Interlude: Guidelines

Guidelines

you must mention what grows
in the rich, musty earth
of your garden
or
dew-speckled leaves, dripping

or
in the kitchen you
(or your lover) must
be seductively slicing
or
rhythmically chopping
or
a pot must be
about to boil over

or
you must mention
your belly
or
your breasts

(bonus points for the adjectives
heavy
or
scarred)

survivors of that
chromosomal misfortune, the
penis, may
refer to it metaphorically only

(bonus points if it's
flaccid
or
a vegetable misshapen
or
a stand-in for weapons of war
but
glorious towers
get the slip
every time)

and
by the way, commas
must always be placed
in the middle, never
at the end of a
line, because
this is poetry, not
just prose
broken up
into bits

and
your chances will improve, if
you spell you name entirely
with lower case letters
and if
you mention your rare
unsigned copy
of

the editor's collection
The Subtlety of Seahorses

(bonus points if you call it
"a gift of words
to a grieving world")

so
these are the guidelines

Submit!

Revisionary Forces

(Or, The Grizzled Veteran Author-Mentor Shares Some Words of
Wisdom with the Freshly Minted MFA Novelist Who Awaits the First
Round of Revisions from the Small Press Copy Editor)

fortify these words
pile the sandbags, reinforce
these syllables, barricade
the theme

see those clouds of dust
in the distance, lad?

the editorial tanks
are rolling in

This Poem Has No Cash Value

CLIP THIS POEM!*

And stampede on down
to the Saddledome Buffet!**

Gather the family and enjoy
Western barbecued Alberta beef,
cowboy beans, salads and dessert
in air-conditioned comfort!

So mosey on down, and bring your appetite!

BRING THIS POEM
AND SAVE TEN PER CENT!***

* poem valid for a maximum of four lunch buffets
(excluding drinks)

from 11 a.m. to 2 p.m. every day of the Stampede

** poem can not be combined with any other offers
and some restrictions may apply

*** poem has no cash value and
must be surrendered at time of purchase

Stop

stop

speak softly
and carry
nothing
but questions

unclench your
right hand
left hand
lips, teeth

exhale
be still, don't
even breathe
feel
the earth tug
at your soles, the
musky air settle on
your skin, saturate
your brittle
bones

no answers
will you hear, but
you will feel your
place

Foreign Affairs

This Sculpture Reminds Me of You

yes, this sculpture reminds me of you
drapery fallen
the truth of things exposed

skin so white and hard and cool
those inverted nipples
that waist that held my fingers
your small sharp nose
and that expression

(I Know Something
You Don't Know)

this museum two thousand miles
twelve million inches
from

(our affair was one of small measures
tiny movements
one step forward, two
steps back

in, but not
quite out again)

twelve million seconds
from
the moment that you
slipped out from under the covers
said goodbye
and disappeared

the bronze plaque warns

Do Not Touch

Spam Filter

How can you ensure
that you will receive
the email
confirming that she loves you
and is not
having an affair
with that guy from her office

        (named Gunther, you think)

while you're away in Vancouver
drinking premium Scotch
and watching strippers undulate
over your face
under the guise
of a trade-show junket?

To prevent spam filters
from filing her love
and devotion-confirmation emails
as bulk
or junk
just follow these simple steps:

* Hotmail, Yahoo, AOL Users:

Click
the Add Address button beside
the From address
at the top
of her last message

(in which she asks you
to remember
to bring her back
some BC wine)

* Users of Microsoft Outlook:

From
the Actions menu

(and you're all about action,
right Big Guy?)

select Junk Email and
add her to
your Safe Senders List

(She is safe, you
can trust her,
can't you?)

* Other Kinds of Users:

Please follow
the service provider's instructions
for allowing confirmation

(that she isn't
at this very moment
in Gunther's office
behind closed doors
giving him something
that to you
she denies)

Glass Half Empty
(Bacchanalian Haiku)

I will swallow this
sadness before it ferments
into bitterness

I will savour the
taste of the lingering pain
of the aftermath

alone in this crowd
I will practice appearing
strong and uninjured

I will drink this glass
empty and wait for myself
to come home again

Six Weeks

he descends the narrow staircase
turning sideways to avoid
little framed pictures
white leather jumpsuit Elvis
Casablanca, *Vertigo*
femme fatale Bette Davis
The Seven Year Itch

reaching for the doorknob
hesitating
looking up

at the top of the stairs
in her little purple bathrobe
An Affair to Remember
she says
remember?

        (inside that ancient cinema
        pink neon flicker
        burnished brass concession stand
        Popcorn Out of Order

        peeling pastel friezes
        a cool, musty womb

she smuggled in a mickey
poured it into the cola
we sucked on two straws
like courting in another era

her sweater threw elections
whenever she
took a sip)

I remember
he says
I remember

Cary Grant
Deborah Kerr
they would meet in six months
atop the Empire State
if their love was meant to be

I can't wait six months
he says
can you?

six weeks, then
she says
and then she disappears

December Valentine

I love you, I adore you
I want to melt into you
when I see you at these parties
across the humming room

as you whistle counterpoint
(thinking no one else is listening)
to the chorus of gossips
and predatory voyeurs
to the pop culture choir
and emotional nudes

I will harden like fresh concrete
when you're laughing with another

explode

        into dust

                and drift

        through

           your nostrils

                and lips

into your lungs
into your bloodstream

to mingle
with your particles

sublimate
and diffuse

still awake, hours later
when all are home and dreaming

scribble on this paper
under windowpane moonlight

because this cannot wait
until February Fourteen
(the day of candy, hearts, and flowers, so they say)

can't have this wrapped in ribbons
can't buy it in a gift shop
this is the message (if I don't throw it away):

I love you, I adore you
I want to melt into you
when I see you at these parties
across the humming room

Storm
(Lavender Blue #2)

out of nowhere there came a storm

> it didn't come from nowhere, really
> it wasn't as surprising as that

> > we're still animals, we humans
> > we feel them coming

> > we just don't pay as close attention
> > as other beasts do

we've got other things on our minds

> but in the back of our heads
> in those unswept primal corners
> we feel them coming

we know

> there is the lull
> that eerie peace
> the silence a vacuum
> temporary

> we never miss the wind so much
> as when
> it disappears

no birds chirp
no leaves rattle
no blurred conversations
from nearby backyards

       then the silence

               slips

                    away

the pink plastic radio
whispers from the kitchen

       Lavender blue, dilly-dilly
       Lavender green
       If I were king, dilly-dilly
       I'd need a queen

hadn't even heard it
until now

rrrrrrrrRRRRRRrrrRRRRRRRRRRRrrrRRrrrrrrrrrrrrrrr.......

fingers of cloud spread overhead like
      bruised, numb digits
      a soldier's hand
      greyish-purple
      swollen
      prepared to destroy

then the whole palm
cups the sky over

tick

a raindrop strikes the glass
we rise
from our purring-cat positions
drawn
to the edge of the screen door

a serious current
pushes your dress
against the tapers
of your legs
strokes the hairs
on my calves, cool
but obsessed
with being noticed
felt

tick
tick tick tick

an unspoken decision
we step through the screen door
let the wind flow liquid
against us, our feet bare and
tentative
on the sidewalk stones

tick tick tick tick

tick tick tick tick tick tickticktickticktickhisssssssSSSSSSS. . .

> drumroll of thunder
> a slow crescendo
> your slender hand finds
> its way into mine

hrrhrrrrrrhrrrrRRRRRRRRROOOOOOOMMMmmmm. . .

(do we tremble slightly?
with delight, anticipation, fear?
or is it just the rumble
pummelling our chests?)

> rain assaults the pavement now
> crackles
> roars defiance
> against the fractured blacktop
>
> hisses upon the lawn
> forcing the blades of grass to bow
> to submit
>
> rumbles like a lynch mob or
> a Victory Day parade

rrrrrrrrrC-CRACKOOOOOOWWwwwwwwwwwwwwww. . .

(Do our fingers, intertwined
grip a little tighter
increase our stake in this
tantrum of nature?)

up above

chain

lightning

        dances

            jagged crazy freedom

       alive

           immortal

           patterns burned

      red

        purple

         then blue

         in our eyes

         when we

            blink

then ducking behind
curtains of cloud,
the dancing lines
of light retreat

leaving behind
only a sprinkling
a small reminder
of what has been

and of what shall surely return again

the air is cool now
almost   sweet to the lungs
reborn

I still have
your hand

and you still have mine

Paint
(Love Song #2)

this kind of paint
has thirty-two colours
and a thousand times more
when you mix 'em together
and maybe an infinite number when
you add black or white (or grey shades)
to the mix

as they age, their tones begin to change
no two are ever exactly the same
some are innocent, primary
some cover guilt
some are contained and can never be spilt
some are green, like gardens and trees
some are red bloodshot eyes and bloody skinned knees
some of the colours can't be seen at all
black moonless nights
and white blinding snow

brotherly, sisterly, fatherly, motherly
pure and forgiving, dirty and ugly
platonic colours, like back rubs from friends
more are like passions, explode on the sand

this place is ours
it belongs to we two
it hasn't been painted
I'm waiting for you

Fortune

these striations
on your index finger
say that you will canoe
past the coal-black banks
of the swollen River Nile

resurrecting Cleopatra
you will steal from her crypt
a precious golden falcon
says this deep line
in the centre of your palm

this tributary
speaks of oil-smoke fingers
from your shattered Sopwith Camel
they reach up to the space
where you fell from the sky

this wrinkle on your thumb
knows she wrapped you in a blanket
fed you chestnuts from the fire
she nursed you and loved you
like an infant, like a lover

in another life
you will see her
passing underneath
a bridge like an arching backbone
and the falcon will fly
from your hands into her nest

the fortune teller whispers
all of this means something else

take her into
the palms of your hands

decode the riddle
and prove your love

Come Back in Time

she turns his palm skyward
he cups the orange streetlight glow
collecting electrons
like raindrops

with her pink fingernail
she traces his lines
sails the tributaries
to deeper rivers

"You've got an old soul," she says

> she sees herself
> in a lipstick-red gown
>
> he's a black-and-white hero
> in his white dinner jacket
>
> visions of spinning records
> golden saxes, beehive hairdos
>
> cool blue jazz radiates
> from behind a violet door
>
> across the street, Motown throbbing
> *Baby, Baby I Love You*

          then they will run
          hand in hand, laughing

          to themselves behind
          suicide doors

          then they will fly
          twin propellers buzzing

          wing tips glinting silver
          We Know Why You Fly

he turns over his hand
grips her pink-tipped fingers

"Come back in time with me," he says

Expedition Frieze

baboons swing in the rigging
fish teem beneath the bow

on deck, jars of clay
precious incense, spices and silk

rigid men in profile
rowing, pulling ropes

the fleet of Egypt in relief on the wall
vibrant reds, regal golds, alive in death

except for the queen who brokered this peace
who offered such riches for trade

her own image razed
by the one who stole the throne

in the Hall of Judgement
the feather outweighs the heart

Interlude: Equations

Equation

it wriggles, it kicks
I stun it with Aspirin
but it throbs in the background
reminding me
that

(a number of crumpled-up pages)

+

(hundreds of minutes I could have spent:
oiling the creaky door
+
scrubbing the coffee-stained tiles
+
cooking Poet Casserole1
+
getting a haircut
+
washing the sheets
+
contemplating the universe2)
+
(one ink-stained right-hand little-finger knuckle)
=

only this

1Kraft Dinner and StarKist tuna
2with beer

Rule of Three

knowledge	wisdom	intelligence
imagination	memory	experience
ambition	compassion	indifference

the difference
in the spaces
in between

speak up	(use your words)	don't mumble
say	(or imply)	what you mean
speak	(or obscure)	the truth

Rule of Three

knowledge   wisdom   intelligence

ambition   compassion   indifference

imagination   memory   experience

                                     the difference
                                     in the spaces
                                     in between

speak up   (use your words)   don't mumble

say   (or imply)   what you mean

speak   (or obscure)   the truth

the truth   the whole truth   and nothing but the
                                      truth

of the people   by the people   for the people

on your mark   get set   go

                                now step away from the mirror
                                turn and face the window

liberty   equality   fraternity

faith   hope   and charity

paper   scissors   rock

Long Division

the big idea, the long view
the passion and the fury

(divided by)

the replacement of the inside joke
you wrote for your lover

(a nice tribute, but
no one else will understand)

the deletion of every adverb
ending in "ly"

(except for suddenly, exactly
slightly, deeply, freshly
surely, neatly, softly
brotherly, sisterly, fatherly
motherly, metaphorically)

the permission that you'll have to get
from the estate of that dead singer

(to use those three small words
that he wrote before you did)

the banishment of the lines you wrote
while drunk or sick or half asleep

(that the editor will arrest
and you will charge with treason
to imprison on another page
for a ceremonial burning)

and then
you carry the remainder

Vapour Trails

›

Rendezvous

this liquid night
an open sky
sanctifies
forgives

here's you and I, this
full-moon searchlight
reveals what we kept
hidden

those guilty whims
now spiral in
lit but seen by
no one

something that nothing
we possess can
contain

when sunrise
discovers
what's been taken
from this space

the harsher light
will puzzle
to identify
the remains

Saturation

that glow on her skin
the taste of salt

that Bordeaux blush
around her mouth

that mixture of tongues
swirling, stirred

that jungle-wild scent
the steam of her heat

mix me a drink
with a taste like that

and I'll be as drunk
as desire is deep

Observations on the Lover's Mindprobe

what are you thinking
right now
she asks me
tracing quaint circles
in the small of my back

it's the question that's sunk me
on other occasions
led to nights of turbulent sleep
and dozens of messages on her machine

so without the usual deliberation, I just say
nothing
nothing at all
not thinking, only feeling

her fingers continue
whirlpool penetration
then she stretches across me
on her baby-powder belly
good answer, she says

Sensory Deprivation

see topographic contours
vertical blind slices
of this world
as you recede
from the bedroom

hear the ringing silence
that once held catlike cries
and then feline purring, and then
the exhalations
of the satisfied

taste longs to probe
divide and linger on
cherry lipstick appetizer
a lick of salty shimmer
delicious citrus juice

touch mourns the loss
of your malleable skin
conducting wistful sculptor's hands
to make a statement
of your curves

but smell the scent that lingers
on this pillow
a reminder

this evening, senses will
come alive again

Vapour Trails

1

follow the scent
of cherry-blossom incense
over terraced fields
with ankles caked in muck

eat rice, drink pungent tea
from cupped hands, outstretched arms

follow a trail of bone-white dust
where the blossom scent grows stronger
than memory
than imagination
through the arched gateway

believe that you hear
every voice of China
singing through the silent haze

inhale the sweet summoning mist
inhale and hold

        within arms' reach
        a girl in golden robes
        you know that you love her
        even before she turns around
        with an incense-burning lantern
        held in her small hands

you reach out
she flinches
the lantern drops, and
the floor is webbed with vines of flame
she turns to
cinders in your hands

2

sweat trickles from
beneath this safari hat

her legs shining icicle tapers
melting from the skin-covered passenger seat

tendrils of heat snake up
from the jeep's open cockpit
phantom tongues of sand lick
at the windshield, she moistens
her finger, flips a page
of a book called
All the Things in Africa I Love

the lioness charges
the plume of dust that follows
will make this
an easy kill

peripheral vision
glance away from the gunsight
see a picture of the lioness
pasted in her book

lower the rifle
let the beast live

claws hollow your belly

teeth shred your throat

before you can ask if there is a page in there
for you

3

awake

left cheek cool
and flat
against the window of
a luxury airliner
on course for something new

somewhere between sleep
and waking
you almost find
an answer to
the question

a stewardess asks
thirsty?
like a snack?
need anything at all?

stretch
yawn
look at the time

and
the question
slips away

These are not Metaphors
                    (These were not Dreams)

above the third eye
in the pensive face that sees
we carved our initials   (you plus me)

between the thirsty roots
two-hands deep
we buried our treasure   (a falcon on a quarter
                            an owl from a box of tea
                            the stones we carried with us
                            the worry doll you made for me
                            foreign coins, domestic marbles
                            pearls from different seas
                            and
                            a silicate sliver
                            from our secret island splintered)

we washed our lucky stones
that we carry with us still
in the stream
that rushes
through the park
in the painting
that hangs
beside the bed
where we
made love   (you plus me)

these are not metaphors
these are not analogies
these are things
we did   (they only seemed
                                          like dreams)

Exit Interview

In your opinion, which came first:
Art or War? Love or Hate?
The Chicken or The Egg?

In your opinion, who was better:
The Beatles or The Stones?

Elvis?
Really?
Elvis?

Uh, thank yuh fo' the lovin', Ma'am
Thank yuh verruh much

What makes you think
I'm mocking you?

What makes you so
damned sensitive?

Do you blame your parents?
Do you blame society?

Whatever, why don't you
pick the next record, then?

Why are you so distant?
Why are you so cold?

If you only had one hour
left to live, would you spend it
with me?

Was it me you were dreaming of
last night?

Why are you lying to me?
Who do you think you are?

Don't you know you're
nothing
without me?

Where
do you think
you are going?

Notes on the Poems & Acknowledgements

Many of the poems in *Six Weeks* had first appeared in various journals and anthologies. My thanks to the respective editors.

"Fortune" was published in the Summer 2013 issue of *Descant*.

"Saturation" was published in a different form as a suite of three haiku poems called "Intoxication" in the anthology *Haiku for Lovers* (Buttontapper Press, 2013).

"These are not Metaphors (These were not Dreams)" was published in the 2013 issue of *The Fieldstone Review*.

"Mixed Tape" was published as "The Recipe (for What We Made)" in *Vallum* 9.1, "Urban Landscapes / Hidden City" (Spring/Summer): 2012.

"Contact," "Come with Me," and "*En Français*" were published in a different form as a postcard story called "Come With Me" in *The Vestal Review* (Summer): 2012.

"This Sculpture Reminds Me of You" was published in *Existere* 31.2 (Spring): 2012.

"Spam Filter" and "Guidelines" (then called "Submission Guidelines") appeared in *Prairie Fire* (Spring): 2011.

"Rendezvous" and "Neon Sin" were published in *Jones Av.* Vol.7, 2010.

"Glass Half Empty" was published in *Carousel* 15 (March) 2004, and also in *2003: Tea For Three* (Cranberry Tree Press) 2003.

"Swirl" appeared in *The Saving Bannister* (Canadian Authors Association, 2003), and again in the anthology *Open Window IV* (Hidden Brook Press, 2005).

"Observations on the Lover's Mindprobe" was published in *The Harpweaver* (Spring): 2002, as well as in *$10 Cash Value: an Anthology of Assets,* (Cranberry Tree Press, 2000).

"Accelerator" was published as "High Diver" in the 2001 issue of *Surface and Symbol.*

"Storm" was published, in prose poem form, in *Canadian Writer's Journal* (Fall): 1999, and also in *Choice Works,* Vol.1, 1999.

A very different version of "December Valentine" was published in the anthology *No Love Lost* (Hidden Brook Press, 1998).

"Invitation," "The Reasons Why" (as "Reasons"), and "Paint" were originally published in the author's poetry chapbook, *Guessing At Madeline* (Cranberry Tree Press, 1998).

"Equation" (then called "Wastebasket Poem") and "Invitation" appeared in *Zygote* (Fall/Winter): 1998 and (Spring/Summer): 1997.

Some poems in *Six Weeks* have won prizes and awards.

"Fortune" was a finalist for the 2013 Winston Collins/Descant Prize for Best Canadian Poem (judged by Mark Kingwell and Leanne Shapton).

A different version of "Vapour Trails," then called "Vapour Trail Dreams," was a finalist for *lichen Literary Journal's* 2003 "Tracking a Serial Poet" contest.

"Stop" won the 2001 Scarborough Arts Council Poetry Competition (judged by poet Robert Priest). "Stop" also won second place in the 2002 New Century Writer Awards.

"Invitation" won second place in the 1998 *Zygote* "Dark of Winter" poetry contest.

"Invitation", "The Reasons Why" (as "Reasons"), and "Paint" were originally published in the author's poetry chapbook *Guessing at Madeline,* which won the 1997 Cranberry Tree Press Poetry Chapbook Competition (judged by Di Brandt).

And also. . .

"Lavender Blue", a verse from which appears in the poems "Storm" and "Neon Sin," is an English folk song dating back to the seventeenth century, which has been recorded in various forms during the twentieth and twenty-first centuries.

"The Luminous Veil" is an anti-suicide barrier that was erected on Toronto's Bloor Street Viaduct. It is estimated that between 60 and 500 people leaped from the viaduct between its opening in 1918 to the completion of the barrier in 2003.

Thanks!
For their abundant love, support, and encouragement, thanks as always to my wonderful family, especially my parents, Mike and Judy Scarsbrook.

For their respective roles in getting this book into print, my heartfelt thanks to Jamis Paulson and Sharon Caseburg at Turnstone Press.

And to all of the friends, students, editors, and colleagues out there who believed. . .
I am grateful! Thank you.